HISTORIC PHOTOS OF
HONOLULU

TEXT AND CAPTIONS BY CLIFFORD KAPONO

TURNER

PUBLISHING COMPANY

Honolulu, 1873.

HISTORIC PHOTOS OF
HONOLULU

Turner Publishing Company
www.turnerpublishing.com

Historic Photos of Honolulu

Copyright © 2008 Turner Publishing Company

Library of Congress Control Number: 2008904905

ISBN-13: 978-1-59652-499-6

Printed in the United States of America

ISBN 978-1-68442-036-0 (hc)

CONTENTS

Sitting to the rear of 'Iolani Palace in this 1880s view, the crater Puowaina is a sacred site that was used by the pre-contact Hawaiians as a place of human sacrifice and *ali'i* burials (chiefs' burials). Rainwater runoff from the crater to the basin of Honolulu helped create the large, freshwater harbor around which the city would develop. Since 1949, Puowaina, or Punchbowl, has been home to the National Memorial Cemetery of the Pacific.

Acknowledgments

With the exception of cropping images where needed and touching up imperfections that have accrued over time, no other changes have been made to the photographs in this volume. The caliber and clarity of many photographs are limited to the technology of the day and the ability of the photographer at the time they were made.

This volume, *Historic Photos of Honolulu,* is the result of the cooperation and efforts of many individuals, organizations, and corporations. It is with great thanks that we acknowledge the valuable contribution of the following for their generous support:

Friends of 'Iolani Palace
Hawaii State Archives
Hawaii State Library, Regional Branch at Hilo
Library of Congress
University of Hawaii at Manoa:
Hamilton and Sinclair Libraries
Department of Economics
College of Tropical Agriculture and Human Resources

We would also like to thank the following individuals for valuable contributions and assistance in making this work possible:

Kathleen Camara
Ritchie Henderson
Markham and Luana Rosehill

This book is dedicated to my five children: Lisa, Cliff, Christian, Lauren, and Aloha, who are the source of my inspiration.

—*Clifford Kapono*

PREFACE

From the time of its earliest inhabitants, centuries ago, the Honolulu coastline offered two contrasting assets of natural beauty—the oceanfront at Waikiki, comfortable for the shallow-draft outrigger canoes used by the native population, and the deep harbor created by the waters of the Nuʻuana Valley, favored later by foreign vessels. The first of these to arrive was the English sailing ship *Butterworth,* captained by William Brown, in 1794. Hawaiians living and fish-farming along the water's edge referred to the bay and its vicinity as Ke Awa O Kou (the harbor of Kou) but Brown called it Fair Haven, a name that stuck when later translated into Hawaiian as Honolulu.

While Kamehameha I solidified a hard-won reign over a unified Kingdom of Hawaii, until his death in 1819, the harbor served a briefly lucrative sandalwood trade and the first stirrings of a whaling industry. Arriving in 1820, New England missionaries immersed themselves in the life of the islands and carved their mark on Honolulu's landscape with small wooden mission houses to which would be added, through their own and their children's industry, large commercial buildings. Between the 1820s and the 1850s, the population of Honolulu grew from about 3,000 to about 11,000 residents. During this time, a number of men with names that would dominate public life in Honolulu for the next century arrived in the islands.

Honolulu's attributes spurred the political interest of European nations and of Hawaii's near neighbor to the east, the United States, which established diplomatic and trade relationships with Hawaii by entering into a commerce treaty in 1826. In 1843, through the machinations of a local British official, Hawaii briefly came under British rule, but the home government quickly renounced the claim and reaffirmed Hawaii's sovereignty. In a speech to commemorate the occasion, Kamehameha III spoke the phrase that would become Hawaii's motto: *"Ua mau ke ea o ka ʻaina i ka pono"* ("The life of the land is perpetuated in righteousness").

In 1850 Honolulu officially became a city and the capital of the Kingdom of Hawaii when Kamehameha III relocated the capital from Lahaina on Maui. This geographical shift significantly impacted the Protestant missionary community, whose members had positioned themselves alongside a ruling class of native Hawaiians, the *ali'i,* as council and spiritual advisors during Hawaii's transition from a feudal society into an internationally recognized member of the family of nations, governed as a constitutional monarchy. The missionaries' direct influence was on the wane, however, and as the years passed those without financial support either returned to New England or settled into the general population of the islands, some to prosper in private business.

Honolulu's importance continued to grow with the whaling industry, requiring expansion of the harbor facilities and government infrastructure. But the shipping trade also brought to the islands diseases against which Hawaiians had no defenses. Consequently King Kamehameha IV and his wife, Queen Emma, lobbied door-to-door to raise funds for a new hospital to intervene in the accelerating depopulation of the native Hawaiians. The hospital was finished in 1859 and dedicated as the Queen's Hospital at Honolulu.

The rapid expansion of the petroleum industry after 1859 eroded demand for whale oil, and the Civil War further depleted the number of whalers doing business at Honolulu. Pro-Union Americans with political influence in the kingdom looked for ways to support the Northern states, and one way was to fill the demand for sugar, a Southern product. Hawaiian sugar became incredibly profitable during the Civil War, earning a competitive place on the world market, establishing an ever more firm hold on Hawaii's domestic economy, and setting the stage for conflict that lay just ahead, much of it to be played out in easy reach of Waikiki and the Nu'uanu-replenished harbor.

—*Clifford Kapono*

Here on the grounds of 'Iolani Palace in the 1880s, King Kalakaua and Queen Kapi'olani stand in the foreground in front of the Coronation Pavilion, with Colonel Charles H. Judd and Antoinette Swan, wife of Lyman Swan, just behind them.

THE LIFE OF THE LAND

(1850–1899)

In 1876, during the reign of King David Kalakaua, Hawaii entered into a reciprocity treaty with the United States to secure favorable terms on sugar exports. A previous attempt to negotiate a treaty had failed, in large part due to Hawaiians' strong opposition to proposed terms that would give the U.S. exclusive rights to the use of Pearl Harbor. The 1876 treaty did not grant those rights, but the issue resurfaced as renewal approached in 1887, by which time an organization of mostly American and European businessmen in Honolulu (some born in Hawaii), unhappy with Kalakaua's rule, were maneuvering to undercut his power. This was done with a new constitution imposed under threat of force by an armed militia.

The new constitution forced Kalakaua into reigning as a puppet of the American influence within his own kingdom. The new government immediately renegotiated the reciprocity treaty, this time granting the lease of Pearl Harbor to the United States. King Kalakaua died in 1891, to be succeeded by Queen Liliʻuokalani. In January 1893, when she announced her intent to replace the 1887 constitution with a new one, many of the same businessmen as in 1887 formed a "committee of safety" and conspired in her overthrow.

The committee contacted the U.S. ambassador and the captain of the USS *Boston,* anchored in Honolulu Harbor, and on January 16, 1893, 162 troops from the *Boston* came ashore. On January 17, a provisional government was proclaimed, and Queen Liliʻuokalani yielded under protest "to the superior force of the United States of America. . . . to avoid any collision of armed forces and perhaps the loss of life."

Whether the U.S. troops landed to actively support the overthrow or to protect American lives and property is a question hotly debated to this day. A hundred years after the fact, during President Clinton's administration, Congress issued a joint resolution apologizing for the overthrow of the kingdom.

The constitution of the Republic of Hawaii was put into effect on July 4, 1894. Four years later, against the backdrop of the Spanish-American War, Congress passed the infamous Newlands Resolution, a joint resolution annexing the republic and former kingdom of Hawaii—a nation with which it had international treaties dating to 1826. In 1900, an organic act established the Territory of Hawaii.

Honolulu's most recognized landmark, Diamond Head, an inactive volcano crater seen here in 1859 from along the Waikiki shoreline, was given its erroneous name by British sailors fooled by calcite crystals that sparkled from it in the midday sun. The traditional name for this crater is Le'ahi (the brow of the yellowfin tuna). Formed an estimated 300,000 years ago, the crater was used as a military lookout beginning in the early 1900s. Named a national natural landmark in 1968, Diamond Head is now a state monument and is used by various state and federal governmental agencies.

In the 1800s, when this photo was taken, Hawaiians relied on Waikiki as an important fishing site, its waters teeming with a variety of fish and lobster available as fresh seafood daily. Canoes like this one would often go several miles out to sea. The large paddle blades served for steering and paddling through high surf.

Built in 1816 along Honolulu's shoreline, the small fort depicted in this painting eventually became a jail for rowdy sailors. It was destroyed in 1857 as part of the harbor's improvement plan but would be remembered in the name of Honolulu's Fort Street, a principal artery running from downtown to the base of the bay where the old fort once stood. In 1968, most of the street became a pedestrian mall.

Queen Emma, born January 2, 1836, was the wife of Kamehameha IV and the founder with him of the Queen's Hospital (now the Queen's Medical Center) in Honolulu. A candidate for the throne in 1874, she lost that election to David Kalakaua but remained committed to humanitarian causes until the time of her death, April 25, 1885. She left most of her estate to the hospital, which she and her husband had founded to combat diseases introduced by foreigners that by the time of its opening in 1859 were threatening the very existence of the Hawaiian people.

Built in 1845, the original 'Iolani Palace was this wooden structure first utilized as the royal palace by Kamehameha III. It was eventually destroyed by termites. With construction of the second and final 'Iolani Palace, completed in 1882 under Kalakaua, a smaller wooden structure would be built as residence for the monarchs, providing them with a more informal setting for their daily living than was commanded by the palace with its rigid formalities.

In 1865, when this view of Queen Street was captured, Honolulu faced many of the problems of a fast-growing city. Overcrowding and random building densities provided opportunity for squalor and disease to spread through certain parts of the town.

Nineteenth-century Honolulu had its own version of the Barbary Coast, with drunken sailors, prostitutes, and cardsharps, and wild cattle running through the streets. The missionaries had influence, but there was a breaking point to every moral regulation they imported. In 1865, when the Tom Moore Tavern was photographed, Honolulu was a dangerous city.

Dedicated in 1874, Ali'iolani Hale was originally intended as a palace for Kamehameha V, who commissioned two Australian architects to design it, but the building was repurposed as government office space before it opened. By then, Kalakaua was king, and Kamehameha V was honored by a tower frieze reading "Kamehameha Elima, Ka Moi." During the overthrow of the monarchy in 1893, the provisional government read its declaration in Ali'iolani Hale. Today the building houses the state supreme court, the state law library, and a judiciary history center, with the much-photographed statue of Kamehameha I in front.

Opportunities in Honolulu in the 1870s allowed anyone with a trade or skill to set up shop and serve the demand for Western products. Many ships' carpenters found new careers in cabinetry and furniture making.

Seen here in all its original splendor, 'Iolani Palace, the official royal residence, was built between 1871 and 1882. The kingdom's last two monarchs, King Kalākaua and his successor, Queen Lili'uokalani, reigned here.

In the distance behind 'Iolani Palace rise the mists of Nu'uanu, its pattern of ridges and valleys creating streams that flow down from this natural amphitheater and continue along the dry coastal flats, eventually reaching the natural harbor of Honolulu. From Nu'uanu, also, the northwest trade winds blow, creating rainclouds along the Ko'olau mountain range that feed the running streams.

The coronation of King Kalakaua and Queen Kapi'olani on February 12, 1883, nine years into Kalakaua's reign, was a significant departure from the ceremonies traditionally attending accession to the royal throne of the Kingdom of Hawaii. The structure seen here, the Coronation Pavilion, was built for this event that melded European formalities such as a coronation ball and state dinner with Hawaiian traditions such as *hula* dancing and a *lu'au*. The celebration culminated February 14 with the unveiling of the statue of Kamehameha the Great that stands in front of Ali'iolani Hale.

Presented to King Kalakaua on the occasion of his fiftieth birthday, these wooden, finely-honed bowls were symbols of power and respect given to acknowledge the king's position in society as *ali'i*.

Waikiki held a special place in the minds and hearts of native Hawaiians. As a traditional place of worship and everyday living, Waikiki, seen here in 1880, provided a means for Hawaiians to maintain contact with the *'aina* (land) with which they felt cosmologically knitted as one. It was not uncommon for the royal families to spend time tending to their farms in Waikiki, as traditional practice dictated, not as laborers but as stewards of the cherished land of their forefathers.

The raw natural wealth of Waikiki can be seen clearly in this nineteenth-century setting from before construction and tourism. As pristine as this view is, the entirety of the Hawaiian Islands was once in this same condition. Fortunately, a few remote corners have escaped the overcrowding and remain undeveloped. What Walden Pond was to Henry David Thoreau, Waikiki is to its people.

Founded in 1858 by partners Charles Reed Bishop and William A. Aldrich, the Bishop and Company bank is seen here shortly after the firm's new building opened in 1878. Designed by architect T. J. Baker in the Renaissance Revival style, the building became a reference point for political and commercial power in Hawaii and the continental United States. Charles Reed Bishop, husband of Princess Bernice Pauahi Paki Bishop, wielded great power in Hawaii but ran his bank, the forerunner of First Hawaiian, with a strong sense of fairness and integrity.

Shipping was a major industry for Honolulu, with tremendous profits to be made along the lanes of the Pacific. But S. G. Wilder, the founder of the interisland Wilder Steamship Company, did not confine himself to oceangoing enterprises. He was also active in the development of rail lines in Honolulu and elsewhere in the Hawaiian Islands. The sign in the shop window at left indicates his business was the local agent for cables and galvanized wire rigging from John A. Roebling's Sons and Company, of Brooklyn Bridge fame.

Clearly there was profit in the cable sales trade and the sundry other enterprises in which Wilder and Company engaged, as evident by this dramatic step up in the size and solidity of its business facade.

The three-story building seen across Honolulu Harbor in this 1880 view housed the sailmaking business of J. M. Oat. His son, J. M. Oat Jr., ran a printing business. Among the younger Oat's publications, he collected and reprinted the *Hawaiian Gazette*'s news accounts of Queen Emma's funeral in 1885

The merchandise broker John Thomas Waterhouse established his import business in 1851. Marketing goods both wholesale and retail, the J. T. Waterhouse firm, operating out of the building seen here at right in 1884, satisfied local needs for everything "from a needle to an anchor" and also did private mail-forwarding in the years before a reliable government postal service had been developed.

Following Spread: The Kwong Hip Lung Company, at far left, was among the many Honolulu businesses owned or managed by Chinese residents. In the background, at right, stands the second Kaumakapili Church, with its distinctive twin steeples. The church was dedicated in 1888, during Kalakaua's reign, but destroyed in the Chinatown fire of January 1900.

普慶戲院

Members of the Kawaiaha'o Church in Honolulu were accustomed to worshipping inside grass huts when, in 1836, King Kamehameha III arranged for construction of a new place of worship. Begun a year later, the coral stone Kawaiaha'o Church, seen here, took five years and the collective effort of more than a thousand men to build. At the church in 1843, Kamehameha III spoke the words that are now Hawaii's motto: *"Ua mau ke ea o ka 'aina i ka pono"* ("The life of the land is perpetuated in righteousness"). King Kamehameha IV and Queen Emma were married at Kawaiaha'o Church, where services are still conducted in Hawaiian.

Tall ships and steam-powered sailboats line the Honolulu waterfront and navigate the harbor in this 1885 view. The large schooners were for heavy, transoceanic commerce; the smaller, steam-and-sail vessels ferried passengers interisland and carried lighter goods. Here, the two steamers heading out of the harbor are, left to right, the *Mikahala* and *James Makee* of the Inter-Island Steam Navigation Company.

To help celebrate Kalakaua's fiftieth birthday in November 1886, incandescent lamps were turned on at 'Iolani Palace, making Hawaii's royal residence the first to be illuminated by electricity. The government followed with an electrification plan for the city as a whole, to be powered by Nu'uanu Valley water. Honolulu's first electric streetlights were in place by March 1888 (switched on by Princess Ka'iulani), and within a year a number of homes and businesses were also enjoying the novel wonder of electric light.

King David Kalakaua's fiftieth birthday was celebrated over many days through festivities held in and around 'Iolani Palace. Kalakaua had a driving passion to revive Hawaiian cultural practices lost to the influence of Western missionaries, while still maintaining a strong affinity for the Western-style education and scientific inquiry he witnessed in his travels around the world.

The tall ships that lined Honolulu Harbor for nearly a century brought building materials and supplies from the West Coast of the United States in exchange for goods such as raw sugar and pineapples. Tall ships built in Oregon, for example, carried lumber from the Pacific Northwest to Honolulu, where many ships would be found loading and unloading at any given time in the harbor. The shoreside labor required was staggering.

Hawaiians with their abstract perspective were fascinated by the written word. Newspapers were a modern marvel that held more fascination than mechanical inventions. The *Pacific Commercial Advertiser,* the ancestor of today's *Honolulu Advertiser,* was founded in 1856 by Henry M. Whitney and was sold to the sugar magnate Claus Spreckels, a royalist, in 1880, or possibly to Kalakaua's adviser Walter M. Gibson. The paper's pro-monarchy editorials were deplored by many resident American businessmen, and the paper was sold to the *Hawaiian Gazette* in 1888, with the combined papers then passing to Lorrin A. Thurston, a leader of the annexation movement, in 1895.

Honolulu owed its growth to the capacity of the harbor to handle trade, much of it passing through warehouses such as this one, viewed in 1890.

The combination of services offered by this business on Fort Street points to the future profitability of a funeral home: furniture, undertaker, and embalmer. The rise in population called for an increase in mortuary services, and perhaps was a factor in the idea put forth around that time to locate a cemetery on Puowaina.

At the funeral service for King Kalakaua in 1891, the grounds are filled with mourners outside 'Iolani Palace, which would stand as his legacy, the only royal residence on American soil and symbolic of Hawaii's era of independence. At odds during his reign with the majority of the American and European businessmen in Hawaii, Kalakaua became a champion of the people, calling for the resurrection of various cultural arts and practices.

Kalakaua's cabinet members stand next to *kahili*s, the black-feathered royal banners signifying the presence of an *ali'i* (king) in 1891. With the king dead, Hawaii found itself in a precarious position. It had never been governed without a reigning patriarch. Queen Lili'uokalani would succeed Kalakaua, but these were the kingdom's last days.

Of all the Hawaiian nobility, Victoria Kawekiu Ka'iulani Lunalilo Kalaninuiahilapalapa Cleghorn, Crown Princess of Hawaii, is one of the most well remembered. As a young woman, educated in England, she fought for the restoration of the Kingdom of Hawaii after the overthrow in 1893, testifying before the United States Congress and pleading her case before U.S. Presidents Benjamin Harrison and Grover Cleveland. Seen here around 1893, Princess Ka'iulani was also an artist. She died in 1899 at the age of 23 years.

William Aeko, one of the
first performers to bring
Hawaiian music to the
mainland, is seen here about
1893, the year he appeared
with a quartet at the World's
Columbian Exposition,
also known as the Chicago
World's Fair. Accompanying
an exhibition called the
Kilauea Cyclorama, the
quartet played stringed
instruments that included
ukulele.

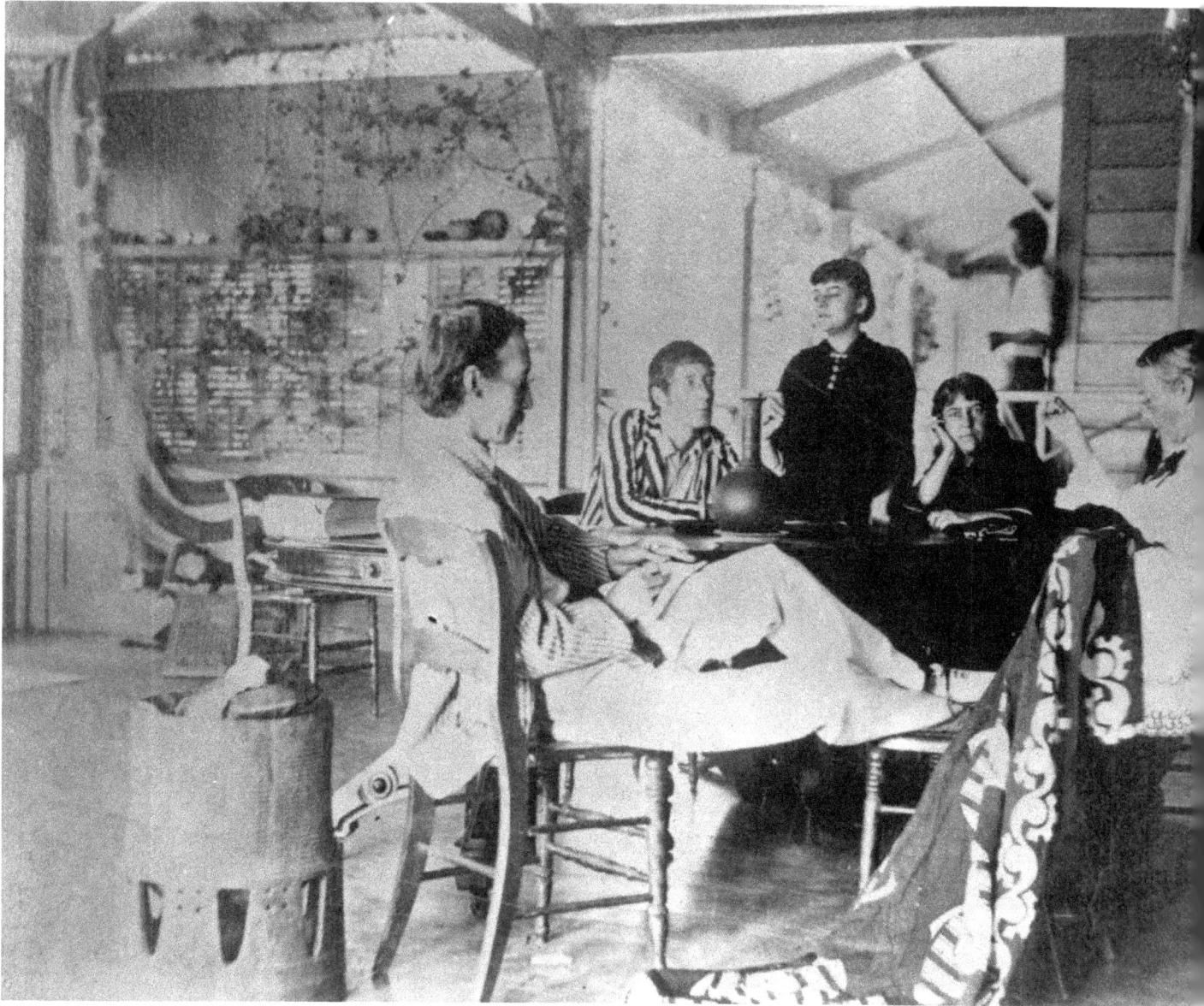

One of many Scotsmen to visit Honolulu was the author Robert Louis Stevenson, who became a personal friend of King David Kalakaua and Princess Ka'iulani while on an extended stay in Hawaii in 1889. Stevenson is seen here relaxing in Hawaii with his family. Princess Ka'iulani was the daughter of Archibald Scott Cleghorn, a financier from Edinburgh who served as O'ahu's last royal governor. While in Hawaii, Stevenson wrote the short story "The Bottle Imp," inspired by the Hawaiian stories he heard while visiting at Ainahau, Cleghorn's Waikiki home.

'Iolani Barracks, or Halekoa (Warrior House) was designed by the German immigrant Theodore Heuck, who was commissioned by King Kamehameha V, and was constructed in 1870. The small garrisons of native Hawaiian soldiers housed there were the reigning monarch's royal guards. During the overthrow of 1893, the small infantry unit would have likely proved no match for the larger, more equipped force of 162 members of the U.S. Navy and Marines that came ashore from the USS *Boston,* had armed conflict occurred.

Bicyclists, barefoot children, and promenaders make the most of a shaded Hotel Street here in the late 1890s.

On Hotel Street in 1898, local Hawaiian flower vendors would set up directly on the sidewalk, where potential customers could walk by and admire the garlands of fresh-strung, scented flower *lei*. For the Hawaiian, a *lei* was a gift of *aloha*. Its significance was in the moment, that for a short time the flower's beauty would enhance the natural essence of the person, and together they were linked to the land, the people, and the universe.

'Iolani Barracks is seen here in 1895. That year Robert Wilcox, a part-Hawaiian in Queen Lili'uokalani's court, organized an armed revolt against the government of the Republic of Hawaii, established after the queen was deposed. Wilcox had led a similar revolt in 1889 against the 1887 constitution that had been forced on King Kalakaua. Both failed rebellions are remembered as romantically courageous, however futile.

Prince Jonah Kuhio Kalaniana'ole and his wife, Elizabeth, are shown here seated in a Quadricycle. Prince Kuhio was imprisoned for nearly a year for his role in the 1895 Wilcox rebellion. Elizabeth Kahanu Woods visited the prince in prison, and they married after his release, in 1896. After a period away from Hawaii, Prince Kuhio returned and served for many years as Hawaii's delegate to the United States Congress.

Seen here on Nu'uanu Street, as viewed from Hotel Street, Love's Bakery was founded by Robert Love, who arrived with his family in 1851 from Australia. A native of Glasgow, Scotland, he started his bakery a month after setting foot in Honolulu. Bakers in nineteenth-century Honolulu primarily served the shipping trade.

In 1888, Hawaiian Tramways Company launched an islandwide transit operation using mule-drawn cars, as seen here on Beretania Street. Making the city more accessible by these railcars allowed people to live farther away from the ocean, in places where traditional housing was built and flourished. As the population moved further inland, water access was a major concern, so the valleys of Nu'uanu and Manoa were often the first choices.

The Coronation
Pavilion at ʻIolani
Palace, where King
Kalakaua and Queen
Kapiʻolani were
crowned on February
12, 1883, is sometimes
referred to as the
ʻIolani Bandstand. The
structure continues
today as the site of
the Royal Hawaiian
Band, which plays
music written by
the monarchs of the
Kingdom of Hawaii,
in particular Queen
Liliʻuokalani, who
wrote "Aloha ʻOe" (or
"Aloha Oe") and many
other Hawaiian songs.

TERRITORIAL TRANSITION

(1900–1919)

The year 1900 found Hawaii under a new, territorial government, with a multiethnic mix of former citizens of Hawaii given blanket United States citizenship—except for the roughly 40,000 Asians living in the islands, most of them working on the sugar plantations, though some had moved to Honolulu. Many of the city's Chinese residents lived in Chinatown, where in January 1900 a controlled fire, lit to combat an outbreak of the bubonic plague, burned through the entire district.

The 1896 census showed 6,327 owners of real estate in Hawaii, and 4,767 of them were Hawaiian or part Hawaiian. No information on individual acreage was collected, because figures obtained in 1890 had been "manifestly incorrect," the report stated. But it has been estimated that by 1900 the ratio of white to native land ownership was four to one.

Honolulu's population in 1900 stood at slightly under 40,000 residents. Irrespective of the shifting political climate, the local economy developed steadily. The Honolulu Harbor facilities were continually improved and expanded through public projects and private initiatives. Hawaiians still favored Waikiki, so there was little attention paid by them to harbor development, even though it was among the forces driving them to near extinction.

The relatively young pineapple industry had a significant impact on the economy, as did construction of a naval base at Pearl Harbor, approved by Congress in 1908 and bringing jobs the following year. The opening of the Moana Hotel in Waikiki and the Alexander Young Hotel downtown signaled an emerging faith in the possibilities of tourism. The territory's economic progress was interrupted by World War I, however, as steamships used for trade and passenger travel between Honolulu and the West Coast were conscripted for service to the Atlantic seaboard. Dependent on ocean transportation, the incipient tourism industry was crippled, and frequent shortages of consumable goods drove the cost of living beyond the affordability of the workforce.

Throughout, the dominant power in the islands remained the sugar industry, by then controlled by a "Big Five" group of Honolulu sugar factors likened then to an oligarchy. As Hawaii's attorney general, a member of the Dole family, described the situation in 1903, "There is a government in this Territory which is centralized to an extent unknown in the United States, and probably almost as much centralized as it was in France under Louis XIV."

Sanford B. Dole was the Territory of Hawaii's first governor under the Organic Act, serving from 1900 to 1903. He was born a citizen of the Kingdom of Hawaii to missionary parents in 1844 and was a cousin of James Dole, the famous pineapple magnate. After the 1893 overthrow of the monarchy, he was named president of the Republic of Hawaii. When the United States annexed Hawaii, Dole was named territorial governor and is seen here being sworn in.

Built in the Renaissance Revival style, the Bishop and Company Building with its arched windows stands behind recently strung wires in this turn-of-the-century view.

The turn-of-the-century waterfront provided jobs that were close to the ocean and to the excitement of sailing ships and new merchandise, and that attracted many to the harbor in search of work. Adults and young children brought their tin lunchpails, ready to work a full day, dressed in appropriate workclothes—coats and hats but not necessarily shoes, which were not mandatory and which many did not wear.

Located at the corner of Fort and Hotel streets, the three-story Mott-Smith Building, at left, was named for John Mott-Smith, Hawaii's first dentist. After arriving in 1851 from California, he also served as a government official and for a time as editor of the *Hawaiian Gazette*. In 1897, a few years before this photo was taken, the Mott-Smith became one of the first two buildings in the islands to boast an electric elevator.

When originally constructed in 1870, ‘Iolani Barracks housed the small number of soldiers who made up the Kingdom of Hawaii's Household Troops. Disbanded by Kamehameha V for a time after the troops seized the barracks in a mutiny, the force was later reconstituted under Kalakaua as the Household Guard, which it remained until the end of the monarchy. Seen here in the early 1900s, the barracks served various purposes, military and otherwise, during the territorial period.

In this turn-of-the-century view of Honolulu Harbor, foreign influence is dramatically clear in the number of tall ships in the distance and the large homes altering the landscape, likely reflecting the wealth accumulated by the sugar barons and those of their society.

These four *hula* dancers were photographed in the crater of Puowaina around 1901. The addition of stringed instruments to Hawaiian music added a new sound to accompany the abstract dancing of *hula*, which contributed to making Honolulu popular with the Western world.

In 1898, the transportation magnate Benjamin Dillingham opened the luxurious Haleiwa Hotel along the rail line he built to serve the outlying sugar plantations, including those of Waialua Sugar Company, of which Dillingham was director. Seen here about 1902, the Victorian Haleiwa attracted Honolulu's wealthy for weekend excursions.

The first Japanese bank to achieve any permanency in Hawaii, the Yokohama Specie Bank (Yokohama Shokin Ginko) was an overseas financial agent chartered by the Imperial Japanese government. Opened in 1910, the Honolulu branch was designed by the prolific architect Harry Livingston Kerr. After the bombing of Pearl Harbor, the Alien Custodian Agency confiscated the bank, leaving some customers to spend years trying to recover their seized assets, on which the government paid no interest until lawsuits long after the fact forced the issue.

Though Hawaiian Tramways Company had operated a mule-drawn trolley line since 1888, the rival Honolulu Rapid Transit Company prevailed in a race between the two to be the first to offer electric railway service to the city. While Hawaiian Tramways rushed to lay double tracks on the streets it already controlled, Honolulu Rapid Transit opted for an electric line from Thomas Square to the King Street Bridge and debuted its service on August 31, 1901. This electric trolley was photographed the following year at Waikiki and Hotel.

Waikiki Beach, seen here around 1904, had always provided Hawaiians with every need they could imagine—food grown in gardens, fish raised in ponds, fruit from trees lining the beach, and endless surf on white sunny sand for idling away their leisure time.

The first hotel resort at Waikiki, the Moana Hotel opened on March 11, 1901, the brainchild of the affluent Waikiki resident Walter Chamberlain Peacock. Despite such modern amenities as telephones in the guest rooms, the Moana struggled initially, and Chamberlain sold it to Alexander Young in 1905, about the time of this photo. Run by Young's estate after his death in 1910, the Moana was sold in 1932 to the Matson Navigation Company.

Hawaiian Electric Company (HECO), whose powerhouse is seen here, grew profitable in part because the electric utility business was so capital-intensive it was difficult to sustain competition. Granted a ten-year exclusive franchise in 1893, HECO agreed to pay the government 2.5 percent of its gross earnings and to provide power wherever requested in Honolulu, though the service remained unaffordable to many. The company expanded the power grid to Waikiki by 1897.

A Honolulu ship chandlery and hardware store, E. O. Hall & Son was established in 1852 and became prosperous providing equipment for the sugar industry, building material for the ʻIolani Palace, power generators for electricity, and eventually even 1,400 gallons of "Eggshell Mill White" paint for the Aloha Tower. E. O. Hall is also remembered for having printed an edition of the Bible translated from English to Hawaiian. A devout Christian, he earned a reputation for being honest and above reproach.

An executive with Honolulu Iron Works and an investor in the sugar industry, Alexander Young parlayed his profits from those endeavors to build the 300-room Alexander Young Hotel in downtown Honolulu, at Bishop and Hotel streets. The building, its interior seen here, cost $2 million and opened in 1903. Two years later Young bought the Moana Hotel at Waikiki.

By 1901, two or three passenger steamers, on average, arrived from San Francisco every week, discharging visitors in need of accommodations. From its opening in 1903, Honolulu's premier hotel was the Alexander Young; at six stories, the hotel was also the city's tallest building until surpassed by the Aloha Tower in 1926.

Seen here around the turn of the century, Fort Street then as now cut through the heart of downtown Honolulu and intersected with Chinatown. In December 1899, the bubonic plague broke out in Chinatown, ultimately claiming hundreds of lives as the terrible disease, often called Black Death, spread through the district's overly congested quarters. Government authorities restricted Chinatown residents to their area or sent them to quarantine camps, then ultimately resorted to a program of controlled fires to contain the epidemic. The first fire was set on New Year's Eve.

On the morning of January 20, 1900, one of the controlled fires set in Chinatown to combat the bubonic plague escaped containment. The fire spread quickly, and soon the entirety of Chinatown was in flames. While their homes and businesses burned, the district's residents were held back from fleeing, due to the plague restrictions. Miraculously, no lives are known to have been lost in the fire, but with Chinatown razed, ill feelings festered as some in the white business community saw an opportunity to expand into the area. This view of Honolulu shows the city after the Chinatown fire, with the shell of the ruined Kaumakapili Church visible at upper-right.

In addition to housing an ice cream parlor, as seen here in 1903, the Elite Building was where the Honolulu chapter of the YWCA rented its first office space after forming in 1900. Completed in 1899, the Elite Building was located on the Bishop Street site of the present Remington College.

The impracticality of long knickers and cumbersome, high-neck dresses still prevailed at Waikiki Beach in this scene from 1902.

This panoramic view from around 1910 shows the sheer scale of industry active on the Honolulu waterfront in the early years of the twentieth century.

Titled "Princess of Manoa," this parade float seen in 1909 celebrates a myth in which a young woman changes from human to spiritual form and becomes the essence of Manoa Valley. Her grandparents also join her in spirit, becoming parts of the valley walls and the shrubbery that grows there. The connection between the people and the land was so seamless that any expression of unity with the natural environment was considered reasonable in Hawaiian mythology.

Baseball was introduced to Hawaii by Alexander Cartwright, one of the game's founding pioneers, who settled in Honolulu after a brief sojourn in the California gold rush of 1849. By 1910, when this photo of a Honolulu team was taken, baseball had found its place as a popular Hawaiian sport.

In 1910 the government went to great lengths to promote Hawaiian flowers in the mainland United States, and also in Canada, Mexico, Europe, and even South Africa, highlighting the whole affair through a lavish floral parade. This particular flower float represents the recently opened Fort Shafter. The float stands in front of the original site of the Kamehameha Schools, built by Charles Reed Bishop to fulfill the wishes of his late wife, Princess Pauahi Bishop, who bequeathed her large estate for the establishment of an educational institution for Hawaiian children.

O'ahu's sugar plantations had their own rail lines to bring sugarcane from their fields to their mills. The first common carrier to connect the plantations to Honolulu Harbor was Oahu Railway and Land, founded by businessman Benjamin Franklin Dillingham. The line was built primarily for hauling cargo but offered passenger service as well.

Founded in Honolulu in 1854 by David M. Weston, the Honolulu Iron Works Company and Flour Mill only briefly focused on milling flour. Like most large Honolulu enterprises of the day, the machine shop grew with the sugar industry, and in 1900 it expanded into a new facility at Kakaʻako. With ship-repair services added to its portfolio, Honolulu Iron Works employed a sizable workforce, as seen here.

Dressed in straw hats, jackets, and long pants rolled up to their knees, these barefoot potential future journalists plied their trade first by selling newspapers and running errands for *Ke Aloha Aina,* a Hawaiian-language newspaper.

Both E. O. Hall and his son William were involved from the outset in the introduction of electric power to Honolulu. As a firm, E. O. Hall & Son sold generators to private homes and businesses before the establishment of a central plant, and William Hall participated in the initial partnership from which Hawaiian Electric Company emerged in 1891.

By the early twentieth century, power lines, telephone poles, streetcar tracks, and picket fences marked the way to Waikiki, along with the endemic coconut trees, which have an average life of 100 years.

Here in March 1913 native Hawaiians reenact the arrival of a high chief flanked by his feather banners, or *kahili,* and surrounded by his warrior men carrying spears, or *ihe.* This type of ceremony is typical of a *Makahiki,* traditionally a four-month period of celebration beginning with the first sighting of the *makali'i,* the constellation Pleiades, in late October or early November. This was the Hawaiian New Year celebration, a time to share and prosper.

In this 1915 view of Hotel and Alakea streets, the humble Honolulu Autombile Stand resides kitty-corner from the majestic YMCA Building.

In this 1916 photo, the streetcar at left is passing in front of Cunha Music Company, an enterprise founded by the songwriter and Hawaiian music ambassador Albert "Sonny" Cunha. Combining ragtime and other mainland musical styles of the day with island music and mostly English lyrics, Cunha helped develop a popular sound that came to be known as *hapa haole* (part white) music.

In 1915 the Japanese Bank of Yokohama opened for business in Hawaii, securing both the consumer banking business of the local plantation workers and, possibly, sugar-export commercial banking. Here in Honolulu the following year, local Japanese residents celebrate the birthday of the emperor.

Living in frequently overcrowded conditions in spartan, clapboard quarters such as these made life difficult for the Japanese plantation workers. Several times during the early decades of the twentieth century, the Japanese workers went on strike for fair treatment by the white plantation owners.

Plantation workers load sugarcane onto carts here in 1917. The sugar industry in Hawaii profited from cheap labor that in the pre-territorial years included contract labor. The Honolulu factors and banks that were connected to this enormously profitable industry became internationally recognized, controlling investments and influencing trade in the Pacific. Under these conditions, sugar dominated Hawaii's economy, influencing government with the same heavy hand with which it controlled its labor force.

Heavily loaded plantation cane cars line up for the round-the-clock milling of cane. Once it had been hand-cut in the fields, the cane was lugged to and stacked on these rail cars by those on the *hapai ko* gang and trundled to the mill. Cut cane had to be processed within an 18-hour window to retain its sugar content.

Bagasse pours into the fire room at a sugar mill in the 1910s. Bagasse is the biomass, or residual product, that remains after sugarcane stalks have been crushed for their juice. The bagasse is often burned to power the mill and has been associated with alternative energy programs, but workplace exposure to moldy bagasse can cause the lung disease bagassosis and in some instances pulmonary fibrosis.

Suggesting the scale of enterprise that linked the sugar industry with the shipping industry at Honolulu, this 12,000-ton steamer is being loaded with sugar from the smaller steamers lined alongside it. In 1919 the average price of sugar was two and a half cents per pound.

Seen here in 1917, the First National Bank of Hawaii opened in 1900 at the corner of King and Fort streets as one of eight banks in Honolulu. Established by a group headed by Colonel G. W. MacFarlane, the bank was to act as a financial agent for the new territorial government. Its first year, the bank reported capital stock of $500,000 and surplus capital of undivided profits amounting to $289,000.

Lydia Paki Kamaka'eha Lili'uokalani, Hawaii's last reigning monarch, was laid to rest after her death November 11, 1917, with a funeral held at 'Iolani Palace. Queen Lili'uokalani reigned from 1891 until 1893, when the monarchy was overthrown by those seeking to institute the Republic of Hawaii. She stepped aside to avoid bloodshed and under protest, expecting reinstatement by the U.S. government. During an attempt by Robert Wilcox and others to restore the monarchy in 1895, weapons were found buried at Lili'uokalani's home, though she denied any knowledge, and for a time she was imprisoned. In her lifetime she wrote more than 150 songs, some of them written during her incarceration.

In 1908, the U.S. Congress authorized a naval base to be built at Pearl Harbor. When construction of a dry dock began the following year, local Hawaiians were concerned about the intrusion into the home of the shark goddess Ka'ahupahau and her brother Kahi'uka, who were believed to live in a cave beneath the harbor to guard against man-eating sharks. Construction mishaps were attributed to violation of the sacred site. After a series of delays, including one estimated to have cost four years and $400,000, a *kahuna* (a native Hawaiian priest) was called to help. After the *kahuna*'s blessing, the dry dock was completed and is seen here at its opening, August 21, 1919.

Officials descend the steps at 'Iolani Palace on June 22, 1918, the day Charles J. McCarthy was appointed territorial governor.

SUGAR, SAND, AND SURF

(1920–1940)

If the 1920s roared in Honolulu, they did so in the oceanfront paradises built to welcome wealthy mainlanders, or on the Matson Navigation Company luxury ships that brought them there. The Banyan tree courtyard of the Moana Hotel and the ballroom of the new Royal Hawaiian Hotel played host to high society and provided another revenue stream for the Big Five firms to tally. The decade saw monumental evidence of those tallies in the architecture of the Bishop Street financial district.

Hawaiian influence on financial affairs was limited to a number of land-trust banks, the largest being Kamehameha Schools Bishop Estate, which continued to hold a large percentage of the land in Hawaii while serving the community and the descendants of the people of the kingdom. By 1920, the number of pure Hawaiians had shrunk to less than 22,000, or 17 percent of the population.

Most of the city's 127,000 residents were left to their own resources. The 1920s opened with a mass strike of the Japanese plantation workers, 6,000 of whom came to Honolulu to ride out the work stoppage. Throughout the decade, the government sought to impose increasingly tight regulation of the Japanese language schools.

In 1926, completion of the Aloha Tower marked Honolulu's waterfront with a premier landmark. The marine industry continued to be the linchpin in commerce between Honolulu and the United States mainland. Ships sent to Hawaii with West Coast lumber returned with sugar and pineapple, provided with price protection from foreign competition and market dominance on the mainland. Hawaii weathered the Depression better than much of the mainland, but all was not serene. In 1938 the dock workers, now organizing across racial lines, went on strike, much more successfully than the plantation workers had in 1920.

In the two decades after Pearl Harbor Navy Yard was dedicated, the U.S. military presence in Hawaii had grown rapidly to include Schofield Barracks on Oʻahu along with several other installations, and a population of 48,000 service personnel by the end of 1940. War in the Pacific inched closer every day.

Construction workers put finishing touches on the Theo H. Davies Building as it nears its 1921 completion. Davies arrived in Hawaii in 1857 and rose from the level of a shipping clerk to build an empire based on interests in the sugar business and, early on, as an original partner with Alexander Young and others in Honolulu Iron Works.

The same Alexander Young who was a partner with Theo H. Davies in Honolulu Iron Works bought the Moana Hotel in 1905. Later, the Matson Navigation Company would expand its holdings in the hotel industry to include the Moana, seen here, which Matson would purchase in 1932.

Light bulbs hang from wires strung beneath the branches of the famous Banyan tree in the courtyard of the Moana Hotel in 1920. Planted in 1904, the tree has since grown to a height of over 75 feet and was selected as a Millenium Landmark Tree by the America the Beautiful Fund in 2000. The Millenium Landmark Tree project was established to protect and preserve one tree in every state.

Prince Edward, Duke of Windsor, heir to the throne of England, sits in a Hawaiian outrigger canoe in the steersman seat, paddle in hand, at Waikiki Beach around 1920.

Wedged between the seawall and a thicket of cars, a large crowd of citizens lines the waterfront for an unidentified occasion in 1921.

Among the oldest Catholic cathedrals in the United States, Our Lady of Peace Cathedral in Honolulu was built on land granted to the Catholic mission by Kamehameha III. Blessed and dedicated in August 1843, the cathedral has long been the focal point of Catholicism in Hawaii, which initially faced strong opposition from Protestant missionaries closely allied with the Hawaiian monarchs. Catholic priests were expelled for a time in the 1830s. In 1839, largely at the insistence of the French government, Catholics were granted the right to worship, and the cathedral land was given.

After imprisonment for his role in the 1895 Wilcox rebellion, Prince Kuhio left Hawaii with his wife, Elizabeth. He visited both Europe and Africa during the ensuing years and fought with the British in the Second Boer War. After returning to Hawaii, Prince Kuhio was elected a territorial delegate to Congress in 1903 and served ten terms, during which time he continued to fight for Hawaiian civil rights. He is seen here about 1920, when he was pushing hard for passage of the Hawaiian Homes Commission Act, a homesteading program intended to benefit native Hawaiians.

Prince Kuhio died on January 7, 1922, just months after Congress passed the Hawaiian Homes Commission Act. This photo is from his funeral at Kawaiaha'o Church. He is interred at the Royal Mausoleum at Nu'uanu.

These one-man fishing canoes, seen around 1922, have the traditional Hawaiian outrigger design that includes a round hull for quick turning—making for a handy fishing vessel along the rugged coast and a great surfing canoe for open-ocean fishing.

The sun sets on the southwest shore at Waikiki Beach. This six-man Hawaiian outrigger canoe seems to be out for surfing on the change of tide. The outside swells are gaining on the starboard side, while the outrigger is strategically placed on the port.

Stories are told that in 1897, the sugar baron Charles M. Cooke and others took their money out of the Bishop and Company bank, by then owned by Samuel Damon, and paraded it downtown in a wheelbarrow before arriving at Fort and Merchant streets, where Cooke and others established the Bank of Hawaii. Giving islanders a sense of wealth, the Bank of Hawaii encouraged personal deposits from the large working-class community in Honolulu and elsewhere. Here the bank interior is crowded for promotional pageantry of some type.

Dressed in a white suit for this event at the Bank of Hawaii is John Carey Lane, mayor of Honolulu from 1915 to 1917.

A German ship captain who settled in Honolulu in 1849, Heinrich Hackfeld operated a general store that grew into a successful trading, real estate, and sugar investment enterprise, later passed on to family members. During World War I, Hackfeld and Company, then managed by George Rodiek, was seized by the American Alien Office Custodian, and its assets wound up in the hands of business rivals who reformed the company under the name American Factors and ran it from this headquarters.

Seen here on a seaplane during his tenure as Hawaii's sixth governor, Wallace R. Farrington, at left, was a newspaperman turned politician who also served as mayor of Honolulu. He arrived from New England in 1894 as editor of the *Pacific Commercial Advertiser*, later affiliating with the *Evening Bulletin*. He was appointed governor in 1921, and during his administration Congress passed the Hawaiian Homes Commission Act, which aimed at returning native Hawaiians to their land.

William Paul Jarrett served as sheriff of Honolulu and of the Territory of Hawaii before being elected a Democratic Party delegate to Congress. Part Hawaiian, born in Honolulu, he took office in Congress in March 1923, about the time of this photo.

During the 1920s, a marked schism in lifestyle existed between plantation workers and city dwellers—including their entertainment options. In this 1924 view of Fort Street, the two-year-old Princess Theater can be seen in the distance, while Victrolas are advertised at left.

Viewed here while under construction in 1925, the ten-story Aloha Tower in its early years was a welcoming harbor landmark and the tallest structure in Honolulu. One of a number of important projects overseen by Honolulu mayor John H. Wilson, an engineer by trade, the tower opened in 1926. Because of its high visibility, the Aloha Tower was camouflaged during World War II.

Crisscrossed trolley tracks mark the corner of Hotel and Fort streets here in the 1920s.

The Ala Wai Harbor, seen here, was created in the 1920s when the firm of Walter Dillingham dredged a canal to flush rainwater from swampy, mosquito-ridden Waikiki. Mayor John H. Wilson promoted a contest to name the new canal, and the winning name was Ala Wai.

Situated in the middle of Pearl Harbor, Ford Island was acquired by the U.S. in 1917 for use in the young field of military aviation. After World War I, the strategic importance of Pearl Harbor grew apace with concerns about Japan's emerging military dominance in Asia. Mindful of the potential threat in the Pacific Basin, the United States began to keep more of its fleet at Pearl Harbor, including these ships seen at Ford Island in 1925.

The typical Honolulu business luncheon has changed much from the time of this scene photographed at the Haleiwa Hotel. Meetings concerning land and commerce issues now include women and Asians, who are involved at every level of the new service economy.

Still under construction here in 1926, the Royal Hawaiian Hotel, nicknamed the "Pink Palace," opened its doors on Waikiki the following February. The hotel was developed by the Matson Navigation Company to complement its luxury steamer service. It was not the first Royal Hawaiian Hotel, however. The original Royal Hawaiian opened in downtown Honolulu in 1872 and was later bought by Alexander Young.

Traveling to Hawaii by passenger ship, well-heeled visitors such as these found their way to the Royal Hawaiian Hotel not by accident but by design of its parent firm, the Matson Navigation Company. No one of the hotel's early guests was more famous than Franklin D. Roosevelt, the first president of the United States to visit Hawaii. During a four-day visit in July 1934 he enjoyed a bit of deep-sea fishing and planted a *kukui* tree on the grounds of 'Iolani Palace.

The sugar barons and other captains of industry created an exclusive society far removed from the average working person in Honolulu. This exclusivity was apparent in every social expression, such as this luncheon held at the Royal Hawaiian Hotel.

Young *hula* girls help decorate a cake taller than they are at the Royal Hawaiian Hotel in 1935.

Aside from the shape of surfboards and the materials used to make them, nothing much about them has changed through the years. The boards are still shaped by hand, and young surfers still ride the waves at Waikiki. This board's flat, round nose and wide tail block were perfect for the south-shore surf. Waikiki has many different types of waves to ride, ranging from small tubes on the inside, like the almond-shaped barrels at Baby Queens, to the larger, full-faced waves found at Canoes or Poplars during a big summer swell.

Those traveling to Honolulu before 1950 came by passenger ship and were accustomed to views of Waikiki from the decks of the Matson luxury ships, or from a couple of surfboards. With the Moana Hotel forward of the Ko'olau Mountains, and Manoa Valley tucked in the background, the northeast trade winds blow onto the sometimes flat surf on Honolulu's south shore. The frequency of smaller surf and gentle waves has made Waikiki a great place to learn the sport Hawaiians are credited with inventing—surfing.

Here on November 9, 1925, the Bank of Bishop's new 75,000-square-foot Damon Building, named for bank executive Samuel Damon, opened at the corner of King and Bishop streets. With the banking business growing in tandem with the sugar and pineapple industries, the Bank of Bishop (formerly Bishop and Company) merged in 1929 with the First National Bank of Hawaii, the First American Savings Bank, the Army National Bank of Schofield Barracks, and the Baldwin Bank of Maui. Renamed Bishop First National Bank of Honolulu, it recorded assets of more than $30 million.

The Bank of Bishop's Damon Building stands in this view with its Greek columns representing strength and permanence.

Seen here at the corner of Merchant and Fort streets, the Judd Building was designed by Oliver Traphagen and opened in 1898. The Bank of Hawaii operated out of the Judd in the early decades of the twentieth century, as did Alexander & Baldwin.

Not long after the Bank of Bishop opened the Damon Building, the rival Bank of Hawaii moved from the Judd Building into this new headquarters.

The Dillingham Transportation Building is seen here not long after its completion in 1929. The Dillingham name had been prominent in Honolulu since Benjamin Franklin Dillingham arrived in the 1860s. He later founded the Oahu Railway and Land Company.

This building was headquarters of Alexander & Baldwin, one of the Big Five sugar conglomerates. The company grew from the nineteenth-century partnership of Samuel T. Alexander and Henry P. Baldwin, both of whom were sons of missionaries. In 1876, in order to meet the heavy water-use needs of their sugarcane fields on Maui, Alexander engineered an irrigation system that diverted water 17 miles from the windward side of Haleakala.

A San Francisco institution founded in 1861, the high-end retailer Gump's developed a strong association with the Pacific Rim. The Gump's outlet seen here in Honolulu featured "hollow tile" in its design.

Heavily uniformed in tropical heat, the policeman seen here directing traffic at the intersection of Fort and King streets needed his umbrella. The Honolulu Police Department was officially established in 1932, though its origins date to government legislation enacted in 1846 under the reign of King Kamehameha III.

The Portuguese introduced the *braguinha* to Hawaii in the late 1800s. The small, stringed instrument caught on like wildfire, and according to one legend, Hawaiians likened the quick-fingered technique of playing it to a *'ukulele* (leaping flea), and the name stuck. The popularity of the ukulele led to a cottage industry with great export potential, especially when a craze for Hawaiian music swept the mainland in the early twentieth century. Here ukuleles are being crafted at a shop in 1926.

On August 16, 1927, shortly after Charles A. Lindbergh made his historic transatlantic flight, a group of aviators took off from Oakland Airport in a dangerous race to Honolulu sponsored by James D. Dole, the pineapple magnate. The team of Art Goebel and William V. Davis, Jr., took home the $25,000 given by Dole as first prize after a flight of 26 hours, while Martin Jensen, of Honolulu, and Captain Paul Schluter received $10,000 for finishing second. Here, Jensen and Schluter's *Aloha* has come to rest at Wheeler Field.

A crowd of onlookers awaits the arrival of the Dole flight contestants. During the race, two planes disappeared over the ocean, as did a third plane that departed the next day to search for them while also attempting to reach Honolulu. In all, ten people died in the Dole race or events surrounding it.

The drama and tragedy of the Dole race, and the adventurousness of the fliers, ultimately helped pioneer safe air travel to Hawaii. The pilot of this seaplane has a clear view of Honolulu Harbor and the Aloha Tower. Looking down, it would have been difficult for him to imagine the growth to come.

The first Hawaiian banquets served at the Royal Hawaiian Hotel were laid out with fine china, crystal, and silverware, a tradition the hotel carried forward when competitive hotels on Waikiki served food from paper plates. This Royal Hawaiian dinner was photographed in 1927.

In the 1920s, the roads in Honolulu were few and not in the best of condition, since most of them were dirt roads, but an automobile like one of these parked outside the Royal Hawaiian Hotel was a necessity for the wealthy.

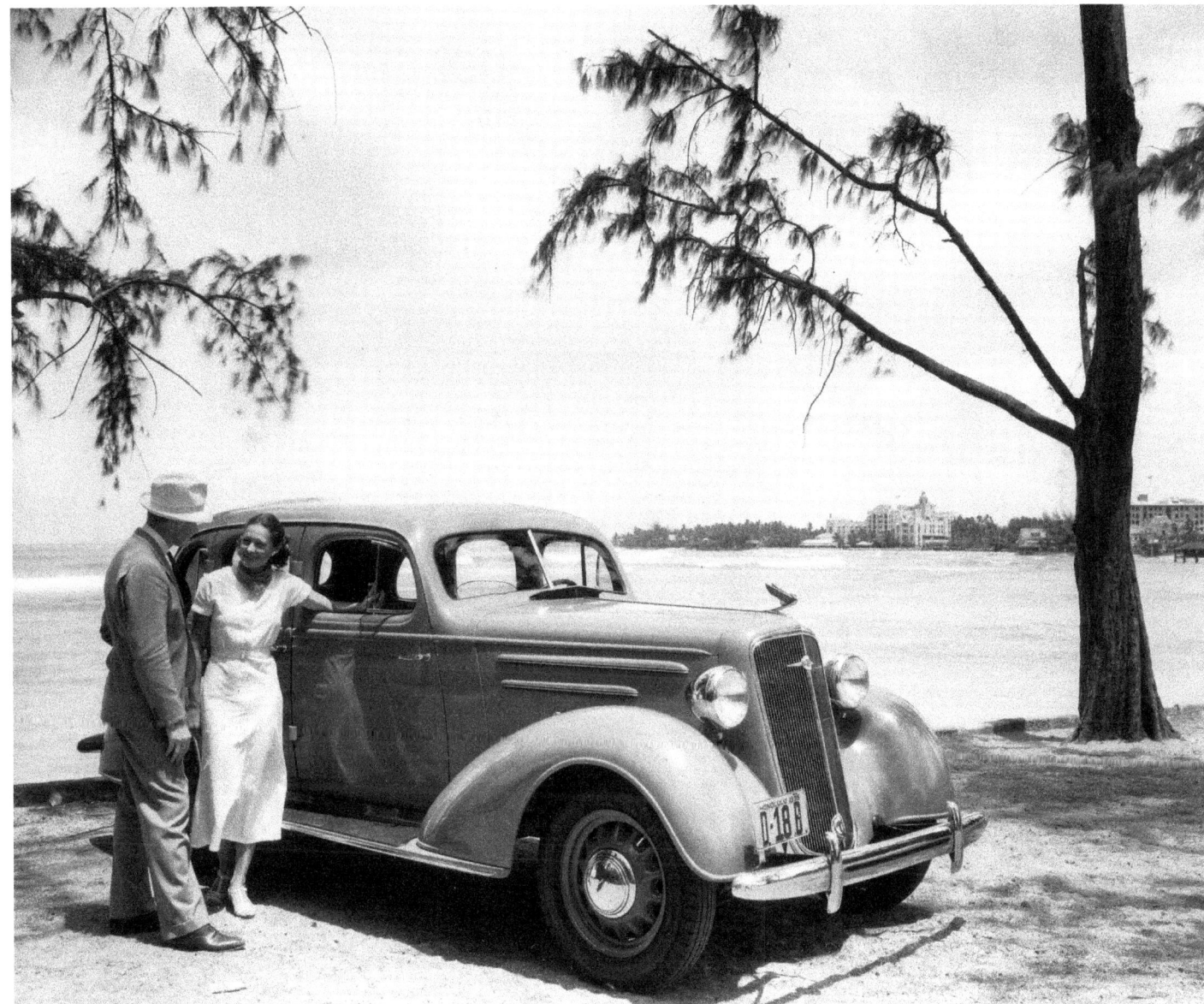

Honolulu has always had a fascination with new things and the latest fashions, cars included. This Chevrolet was a popular model of the times; today, fancy imports and high-end luxury cars are seen all over Honolulu, most stuck in traffic.

Seen here in 1930, these are the famous Waikiki beach boys, acclaimed for their expert waterman skills and their charm, who plied their trade on the beach fronting the Royal Hawaiian and Moana hotels. Teaching visitors to surf, catch waves in outrigger canoes, and enjoy the easygoing Hawaiian culture, they became unofficial ambassadors, adding to the mystique and glamour of Hawaii's travel industry.

The Pearl Harbor Navy Yard is seen here at its entrance in the 1930s, by which time the facility included an air station and a submarine base.

In 1934 a schoolboy looks out over Honolulu from atop Puowaina, where marked stones indicate the distances to various landmarks. By then Honolulu was no longer an isolated spot on an island out in the middle of the Pacific Ocean. In three fast decades since annexation the city had grown into a major U.S. port with a sizable military presence. Some residents saw Honolulu as continuing to provide the prosperity that they and their families had long known; for others, it was still a servant's perspective. Either way, the view had become more interesting than ever.

Cars follow a trolley down King Street in 1934, a year notable, among other milestones, for the election of Duke Kahanamoku, the Olympic gold medalist and surfing popularizer, to the office of sheriff of Honolulu.

As a Honolulu industry, skipjack tuna fishing grew from the level of local-market commerce to eventually supply the Hawaiian Tuna Packers cannery, where this hardworking tuna packer probably was photographed.

Founded by Gustav Schuman in 1893, the venerable Schuman Carriage sold horse-drawn buggies and carriages, but rather than be left behind by the horseless carriage, Schuman introduced the new contraption to Hawaii and thrived in auto sales; the Honolulu firm he started remained in business for more than a century.

Many Japanese laborers started small businesses in Honolulu, as did many Chinese. Some succeeded in much larger enterprises. The grandson of a Chinese immigrant, Chinn Ho was born in Waikiki and eventually became a self-made multimillionaire, developing the Ilikai hotel-condominium high-rise and becoming the first Asian director of the Big Five firm Theo H. Davies and Company.

Located by the harbor, the Dillingham Transportation Building glows at night in 1934, five years after its completion.

Despite the Depression and the large sums of money kept in the banks here on Bishop Street, Hawaii saw no bank robberies until February 3, 1934—and that took place at a Bank of Hawaii branch on Maui. The robbers were quickly caught and were sentenced to 20 years in prison. Most of the money they stole, slightly more than $975, was recovered.

The pilot Sir Charles Kingsford Smith, at right, and co-pilot Charles Ulm, at left, landed in Honolulu in 1934 on their way to Australia. In 1928 the two had made the historic first transpacific flight from the United States to Australia, a three-part journey during which they stopped in Hawaii.

Seen here in 1935, the Kress Building stood on Fort Street. Samuel H. Kress, founder of the Kress five-and-ten-cent store chain, donated a portion of his art collection to the Honolulu Academy of Arts. The museum, which opened in 1927, was founded by Anna Rice Cooke, wife of the politician and businessman Charles M. Cooke.

Seen here in 1935, the Arnott and Hough auto repair shop specialized in fixing Studebakers.

A variety of sturdy cars line Bishop Street in 1935. Honolulu developed a large automobile population rapidly, in part because to an island consciousness the idea of mobility was powerfully liberating. One benefit of having a car was the broader range of entertainment options it provided.

The beach provided the perfect setting for reading, and no doubt the tourists who came to Waikiki long before the days of floor shows, restaurants, and nightclubs had little to do but relax with a favorite book during the day and walk the white sands by night.

This 1935 scene of sail-rigged outrigger canoes along Waikiki is unusual. The Hawaiian outrigger canoe is designed to make quick turns and navigate along the coast, by evidence of its round hull and lack of a keel. The steering paddle serves as rudder and keel while the outrigger to leeward provides a stable course. The steersman must keep a watchful eye on the position of the outrigger and sail relative to the ocean swell. This is not an easy task, and because the canoes are small they are very unforgiving.

Another Big Five firm with a bewildering array of holdings (including most of the island of Lanaʻi), Castle & Cooke was started by Samuel N. Castle and Amos S. Cooke, both of whom arrived in Hawaii in 1837 to do mission work and who started their business partnership in 1851. The company building is seen here in 1938, not long after Castle & Cooke had acquired a controlling interest in James Dole's Hawaiian Pineapple Company.

Throughout the 1930s, Hawaii's military population was on the increase, as can be seen by the number of servicemen walking past Honolulu Sporting Goods here in 1936. Their growing presence provided local residents with opportunity for a wider exposure to American culture. The military represented chivalry and honor, making it an admired profession for many Hawaiians.

The superstar actor and singer Bing Crosby visited Hawaii prior to starring in the 1937 film *Waikiki Wedding*, which was mostly filmed in California but featured Crosby singing "Sweet Leilani," a song he first heard played at the Royal Hawaiian Hotel in Honolulu. Written by Royal Hawaiian bandleader Harry Owens upon the birth of his daughter, "Sweet Leilani" won the Oscar for best original song. Crosby recorded the hit tune accompanied by Lani McIntire & His Hawaiians.

Fascination with Waikiki as an ultimate tourist destination affected the movie stars of the time. Here Betty Compson, a Hollywood star who had done some silent-film work in Hawaii in the 1920s, poses at the beach. Honolulu would become a second home to many movie stars and celebrities. In addition, the amount of filmmaking done in the islands through the years would help establish a small film industry, providing employment for local actors and writers.

Like banks did on Bishop Street, retailers lined Fort Street in 1938. People in Hawaii fared better than most during the Depression, mainly because demand for sugar was constant and labor was needed. Even so, Royal Credit Jewelers apparently determined that the only way to sell jewelry in Honolulu was on credit.

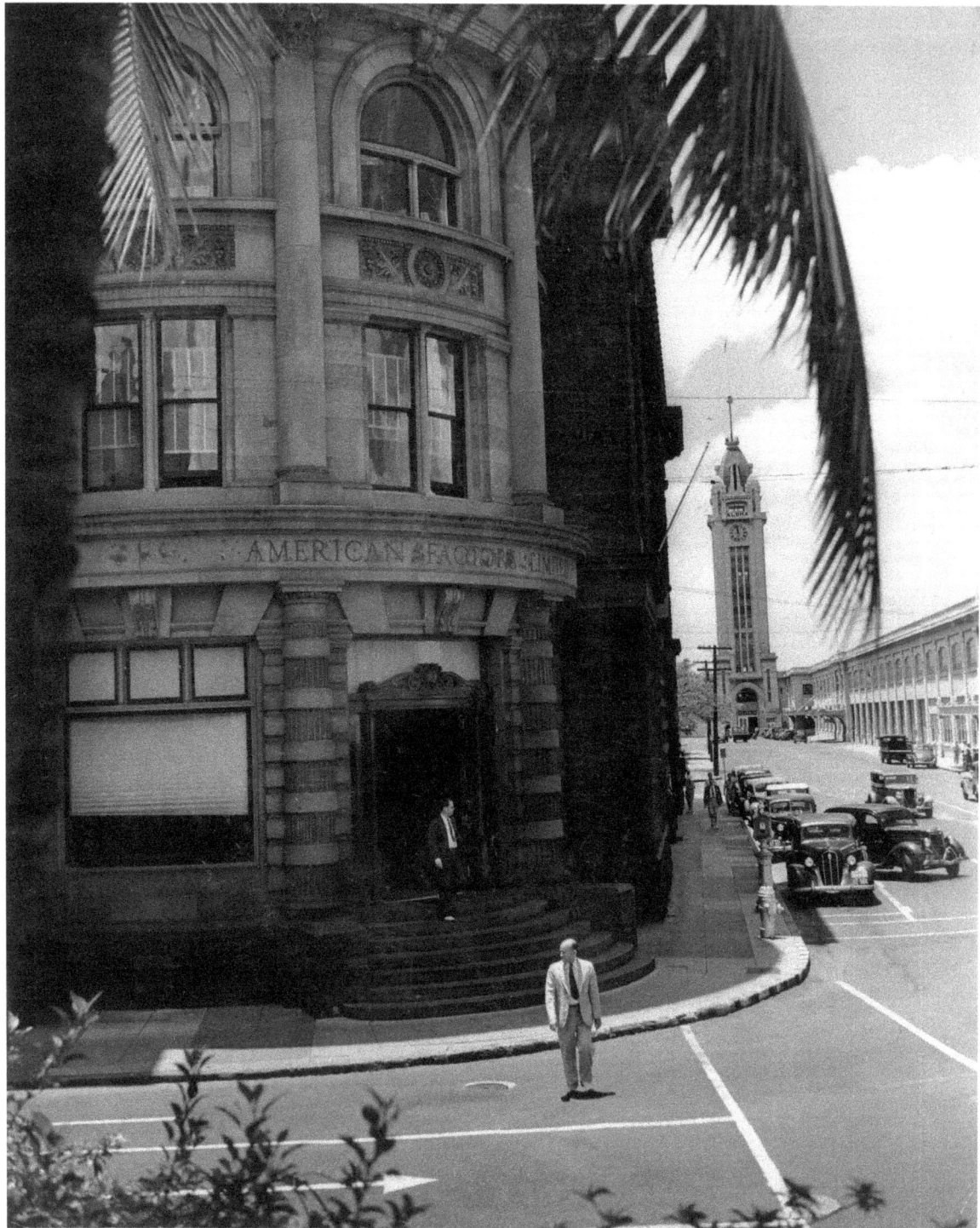

Seen here in 1939, the American Factors Building housed the Big Five company later known as Amfac. Among its many enterprises, American Factors was longtime parent company of the Liberty House retail chain.

PEARL HARBOR AND AFTER

(1941–1970)

The destruction wrought by the Japanese sneak attack on Pearl Harbor on December 7, 1941, was of a scale unimaginable beforehand: 2,403 American lives lost, including 68 civilians. Twenty-one ships sunk or damaged, 347 aircraft destroyed or damaged.

In Honolulu, the impact was felt in a multitude of ways. The city mourned as the dead were buried in local cemeteries. Tens of thousands of women and children were evacuated from the islands. Martial law was declared, with Christmas a military-ordered workday. Fears of a follow-up attack were pervasive. The beach at Waikiki was strung with barbed wire to deter invasion. Small Japanese submarines lurked offshore, threatening the island harbors and sinking Matson ships at sea, with many crew members killed or wounded.

Questions arose immediately about the loyalty of the 160,000 Japanese living or born in Hawaii, and over time more than 1,000 were arrested. But others, committed to fighting as Americans, served with great distinction and sacrifice as members of the 100th Infantry Battalion (Separate) and the 442nd Infantry Regiment.

The end of the war brought much change and opportunity. Soldiers of the 100th and the 442nd, having fought for the United States, now demanded a place as Americans in the future of Hawaii. The Big Five looked forward to supplying a broader range of goods and services in the rebuilding of the Pacific, while postwar trade through the Honolulu Harbor and tourism at Waikiki accelerated. A newly energized Democratic Party won its first ever majority in the territorial legislature in 1954. Hawaii's workers supported the Democrats, but labor gains were forestalled by charges of communism leveled against prominent union members and others. Seven people were eventually convicted of violating the Smith Act, though their convictions were later overturned.

Native Hawaiians desiring independence found hope in the language of the United Nations charter's "Declaration Regarding Non-Self-Governing Territories." As it turned out, Hawaii's postwar direction was to statehood. In the plebiscite of June 27, 1959, eligible voters chose by a 17–1 margin to join the Union as the fiftieth state. Among 240 precincts, the only holdout to vote against statehood was Niʻihau, a remote island with a majority population of native Hawaiians.

Before dawn on December 7, 1941, when the Japanese attack began, eight of the nine battleships in the United States Navy fleet were anchored at Pearl Harbor. USS *California*, USS *Maryland*, USS *Oklahoma*, USS *Tennessee*, USS *West Virginia*, USS *Nevada*, and USS *Arizona* were positioned along Battleship Row. USS *Pennsylvania* was in dry dock.

Moored outboard of the *Maryland*, the *Oklahoma* was hit by torpedoes repeatedly and keeled over, sinking in the harbor. More than 400 of the *Oklahoma* crew were killed, many of them trapped in the overturned hull. Rescue personnel were able to cut free 32 of the men.

In dry dock astern of the badly hit destroyer USS *Downes* and the capsized destroyer USS *Cassin,* the *Pennsylvania,* flagship of the fleet, survived the attack with minimal damage and would be back in service within months.

The Japanese attack targeted the nearby airfields, along with the Pearl Harbor Navy Yard. At Hickam Army Airfield, two-thirds of the bombers on the ground sustained crippling damage. The barracks was also hit, killing many. Few U.S. aircraft managed to get airborne during the attack, but those that did were able to shoot down a number of Japanese planes; in the chaos, some U.S. fighters came under fire from American antiaircraft gunners.

The sneak attack of December 7, 1941, and the continued attacks on Hawaii as late as March of 1942 preyed heavily on the minds of those living in Honolulu. Fearful that the Japanese might invade Hawaii, many residents made plans for evacuation on ships leaving for the West Coast.

Sailors and civilians fill the streets outside the Hawaiian Electric Company headquarters. After Pearl Harbor, with electric power being so vital to defense, the territorial government spent $300,000 securing HECO power plants against further attacks. During the war, HECO plants delivered as much as a million kilowatt hours of electricity on any given day.

Civilians and military personnel wait at a bus stop in 1943. Many Americans stationed in Hawaii would return to live in Honolulu after the war.

In a contrasting view from 1943, the Honolulu streets are virtually deserted.

On May 21, 1944, a second disaster at Pearl Harbor during World War II occurred at the West Loch Naval Magazine. A munitions explosion on one of 29 LST landing ships that had anchored at West Loch triggered a chain of fires on the nearby ships, ultimately killing 163 men and wounding 396. The LSTs were headed for the invasion of Saipan; in order to maintain the secrecy of their mission, the disaster at West Loch was kept quiet.

Here in 1944, with sidewalks full in the downtown shopping district, Honolulu could be mistaken for any peacetime city on a warm Saturday afternoon. In fact, Hawaii remained under martial law until October that year, as it had been since hours after the attack on Pearl Harbor.

The surrender of Japan in August 1945 was celebrated throughout the United States, but the celebration held a particular poignancy in Honolulu. The end of the war would bring new opportunities to everyone in Hawaii, but the dominant question looming would be the future status of Hawaii itself.

Curiously, the last of the classic Big Five headquarters to be built, the C. Brewer Building, completed in 1930, housed the oldest of the Big Five firms. The company's roots dated to 1826, when Captain James Hunnewell of Massachusetts entered the sandalwood trade. After Captain Charles Brewer joined him as a partner in 1836, C. Brewer and Company shifted its focus to the whaling industry, then, inevitably, to sugar.

In this 1947 aerial view, one can see clearly the enormity of Nuʻuanu Valley and picture how the water would flow into what became known as Honolulu Harbor. The carved valley walls act like flumes, sending captured rainwater into the harbor.

This residential street near Waikiki Beach indicates how much the area had been developed by the 1940s. As the beach grew in demand, the local people moved further back away from the shoreline.

The financial power concentrated on Bishop Street here in 1948 owed much to a century of sugar production, but in the years after the war the Big Five would look to further diversify their holdings and accelerate their investment in tourism.

Like transit companies everywhere, Honolulu Rapid Transit found its trolley line aging and outmoded by the 1930s, and so began to offer bus service. But the company had agile competition in the form of small jitneys, so in 1940 the territorial public utilities commission granted Honolulu Rapid Transit a monopoly as a common carrier, forcing the popular jitney services to cease operation. Here, some years later, moving a fleet of Honolulu Rapid Transit buses is all in a day's work for these waterfront freight-handlers.

Popular with the Hawaiian community, the coconut served many purposes, including adaptation for use as a fishing buoy or portable water container. Dried, its shell could hold fishing hooks or be cut in half to serve as a cup. The outer husk of the coconut could be burned, and the ash was often used as a dye. Nevertheless, though a small industry existed, coconuts were never cultivated in Hawaii on a scale to compete with sugarcane and pineapples.

Traditionally, Hawaiians didn't wear broad-billed hats. When the sun was too hot, they simply sought shelter. It was plantation work that called for protection from the sun during the long hot hours in the fields, and so out of necessity coconut hats such as these were weaved and later became popular with tourists. A Hawaiian could weave a coconut hat in a matter of minutes, sized to fit.

Apparently merchants in the 1940s in Honolulu ignored clothes hangers; everything was folded and put on shelves, giving their wares the sense of a more personal touch.

The opening of a Sears, Roebuck retail outlet on Beretania Street in 1941 augured larger changes to come in the postwar Honolulu business environment. Competing with American Factors' Liberty House retail chain, Sears set an example for other mainland firms by making inroads into the Big Five's domain.

Shoppers peruse the goods at the Sears store in Honolulu.

A pose is struck on the beach in front of the Halekulani Hotel, which first opened as a residential hotel in 1907. Though it has undergone many changes through the years, one thing that hasn't changed is that the Halekulani is still well known for its coconut cake.

This beach fronted the famous Queen's Surf, a popular nightclub of the 1950s and 1960s. Owned by the Weaver brothers, Spence and Cliff, the club attracted local beach boys as well as tourists, and featured prominent Hawaiian musicians such as the slack-key guitar virtuoso Philip "Gabby" Pahinui. In a famous episode in Honolulu politics, Mayor Frank Fasi, feuding with the Weavers, ordered the Queen's Surf closed on December 31, 1969, a decision delayed a few months in the courts but ultimately upheld.

One of three high-rise hotels to open on Waikiki in the year 1955 (the others being the Princess Kaiulani and the Reef), the Waikiki Biltmore, seen here, surpassed the Aloha Tower in height.

Honolulu in December 1950 was winter like anywhere else in the northern hemisphere—except for the 80-degree temperatures, balmy trade winds, and occasional showers. With Christmas decorations overhead offering season's greetings, shoppers jam downtown Honolulu looking for that special gift.

Opened as a hotel in 1903, the mammoth Alexander Young Building is seen here in 1952, by which time the size of Hawaii's tourism industry had advanced quite a bit from the 2,000 visitors who arrived at the islands the building's first year.

Shown here being sworn in as governor of Hawaii on February 28, 1953, Samuel Wilder King was appointed to the office by President Dwight D. Eisenhower. King had earlier served as chairman of the Hawaii Statehood Commission.

This aerial photo of Honolulu in 1953 provides an overhead view of the large financial institutions clustered on treeless Bishop Street.

On May 6, 1948, Maurice Sullivan and the Lau Kun family together introduced the modern, postwar supermarket concept to Honolulu when they opened Foodland at Market City. The lot is full outside Foodland here in 1953.

The traffic congestion at Fort and King streets in 1955 suggests the pressures on Honolulu's infrastructure as Hawaii's transition to statehood approached.

In 1955 the urban sprawl of Honolulu was reaching to all sides of the island, as suggested by the volume of traffic winging down the Nimitz Highway. That year, with airplanes supplanting passenger ships for travel to Waikiki, the Hawaiian Aeronautics Commission announced plans for a $7 million remodeling and runway extension to improve capacity at the Honolulu Airport.

Palm trees wave in front of the Castle & Cooke Building in the 1950s.

H. F. Wichman and Company, seen here, was a Honolulu jewelry business founded by Henry F. Wichman in the late nineteenth century.

Waikiki's south shore holds some of the best water for surfing anywhere in the world. Known for its gentle waves and soft juice, Waikiki is a collection of inside and outside reef breaks, depending upon the size of the swells rolling in. Credited with inventing the sport of surfing, Hawaiians fashioned long flat planks of hard wood for sliding along the water, calling the practice *he'e nalu* (sliding on waves).

The introduction of American mainstream culture influenced the diets and social pastimes of the islanders. Woolworth's, seen here, captured the attention and appetites of many with soda fountain food and traditional local favorites. Eating alongside strangers in these new casual formats fostered the spirit of *aloha*, bringing a sense of hospitality that grew into a reputation that Hawaii became famous for.

For all the impact of stores like Sears, shopping in the 1950s still centered on the basics. Yardage was a popular product used for making dresses and shirts. Here, locals curious about new goods from the mainland wait patiently in line to make their purchases.

The soft white sands of Waikiki make for pillowlike chairs for this crowd looking toward the water, perhaps watching a Hawaiian outrigger canoe race.

By 1959, business activity at the Alexander & Baldwin Building had begun to shift into lucrative new ventures such as real estate development.

The calm of this scene on Fort Street in 1959 belies the year's drama, as Hawaii voted for statehood.

While Inter-Island Airways had made its first scheduled flight as far back as November 1929, the interisland transportation market grew with statehood and the rapidly expanding tourist industry, involving both established carriers and small commuter planes.

With Diamond Head still offering a dramatic backdrop, the recent changes to Waikiki in the 1960s can be seen in the number of high-rise buildings visible in this aerial view.

After World War II, the continued presence of the Pearl Harbor Navy Shipyard, seen here from above in the 1960s, provided employment and a source of economic stability to the region, in addition to being an ever-present reminder of the sacrifices made there.

The natural beauty of Waikiki, where nature placed trees like these along the white sandy beach highlighted by the mountain Leʻahi in the background, explains perfectly why the Hawaiians when they first reached this place were content to stay forever.

Notes on the Photographs

These notes, listed by page number, attempt to include all aspects known of the photographs. Each of the photographs is identified by the page number, photograph's title or description, photographer and collection, archive, and call or box number when applicable. Although every attempt was made to collect all available data, in some cases complete data was unavailable due to the age and condition of some of the photographs and records.

II — HONOLULU, 1873
Courtesy of Hawaii State Archives

VI — 'IOLANI PALACE AND PUOWAINA
Courtesy of Hawaii State Archives

X — OUTSIDE 'IOLANI PALACE
Courtesy of Hawaii State Archives

2 — DIAMOND HEAD
Courtesy of Hawaii State Archives

3 — HAWAIIAN CANOE
Courtesy of Hawaii State Archives

4 — FORT AT HONOLULU
Courtesy of Hawaii State Archives

5 — QUEEN EMMA
Library of Congress 02017u

6 — ORIGINAL 'IOLANI PALACE
Courtesy of Hawaii State Archives

7 — VIEW OF QUEEN STREET
Courtesy of Hawaii State Archives

8 — TOM MOORE TAVERN
Courtesy of Hawaii State Archives

9 — ALI'IOLANI HALE
Courtesy of Hawaii State Archives

10 — M. T. DONNELL CABINET MAKER AND UPHOLSTERER
Courtesy of Hawaii State Archives

11 — 'IOLANI PALACE
Courtesy of Hawaii State Archives

12 — MISTS OF NU'UANU BEHIND 'IOLANI PALACE
Courtesy of Hawaii State Archives

13 — CORONATION PAVILION
Courtesy of Hawaii State Archives

14 — ROYAL WOODEN BOWLS
Courtesy of Hawaii State Archives

15 — WAIKIKI
Courtesy of Hawaii State Archives

16 — WAIKIKI
Courtesy of Hawaii State Archives

17 — BISHOP AND COMPANY
Courtesy of Hawaii State Archives

18 — WILDER STEAMSHIP COMPANY
Courtesy of Hawaii State Archives

19 — WILDER AND COMPANY BUSINESS FACADE
Courtesy of Hawaii State Archives

SELECTED BIBLIOGRAPHY

This book has benefited from information provided in a multitude of print and online sources. The following were particularly helpful:

Bacchilega, Cristina. *Legendary Hawai'i and the Politics of Place: Tradition, Translation, and Tourism.* Philadelphia: University of Pennsylvania Press, 2006.

Daws, Gavin. *Honolulu the First Century: The Story of the Town to 1876.* Honolulu: Mutual Publishing Company, 2006.

Daws, Gavan. *Shoal of Time: A History of the Hawaiian Islands.* New York: Macmillan Company, 1968.

Kuykendall, Ralph S. *The Hawaiian Kingdom: Volume 1: 1778–1854: Foundation and Transformation.* Honolulu: University of Hawaii, 1938, 1965.

Kuykendall, Ralph S. *The Hawaiian Kingdom: Volume II: 1854–1874: Twenty Critical Years.* Honolulu: University of Hawaii, 1953.

Kuykendall, Ralph S. *The Hawaiian Kingdom: Volume III: 1874–1893: The Kalakaua Dynasty.* Honolulu: University of Hawaii, 1967.

Merry, Sally Engle. *Colonizing Hawai'i: The Cultural Power of Law.* Princeton: Princeton University Press, 2000.

Various. "150 Years of Hawai'i's History." *Honolulu Advertiser*, series: July 2, 2006. http://the.honoluluadvertiser.com/150

Various. "Hawaii Looking Back: A Retrospective on the Cusp of the New Millennium." *Honolulu Star-Bulletin*, series: May 5–November 8, 1999. http://archives.starbulletin.com/specials/millennium/index.html.

"History of Oahu's Harbors." State of Hawaii Department of Transportation, Harbors Division. http://www6.hawaii.gov/dot/harbors/oahu/history.htm.

HISTORIC PHOTOS OF
HONOLULU

From the outrigger canoes of Waikiki to the tall ships of Honolulu Harbor, from the Kingdom of Hawaii to statehood, the history of Honolulu through good times and bad has always played out against a backdrop of uncommon natural beauty. Home to the only royal residence on American soil, Honolulu witnessed in less than a century's time the overthrow of the Hawaiian monarchy, the rise of the powerful sugar barons, an outbreak of bubonic plague, and the devastating attack on Pearl Harbor. Yet always this unique port city has offered an easygoing, welcoming spirit, along with the warm trade winds and soft ocean swells for which Honolulu is world famous.

Historic Photos of Honolulu presents nearly 200 images from the later years of the Hawaiian kingdom to the early years of the fiftieth state. Reproduced in vivid black and white, the photos in this volume show the city's evolution and change, yet with a sense of its uncommon beauty ever present.

Clifford Kapono is a native Hawaiian who brings to the subject of Honolulu history a voice from the perspective of Hawaii's first people, and an informed view of Hawaii's transition from a traditional tribute economy to that of the twenty-first century. He is a graduate of San Francisco State University, with advanced study at Dartmouth College and the University of Hawaii. This is his first book.

WWW.TURNERPUBLISHING.COM

www.ingramcontent.com/pod-product-compliance
Lightning Source LLC
Chambersburg PA
CBHW061228150426
42812CB00054BA/2541